The Pony Express

by Phillip Wright
illustrated by Audrey Durney

Core Decodable 89

McGraw Hill Education

Bothell, WA • Chicago, IL • Columbus, OH • New York, NY

MHEonline.com

Send all inquiries to:
McGraw-Hill Education
8787 Orion Place
Columbus, OH 43240-4027

ISBN: 978-0-02-132383-8
MHID: 0-02-132383-6

Printed in the United States of America.

7 8 9 LCR 25 24 23

Tony looked at photos. "What was the Pony Express?" he asked Mom.

Mom smiled. "In old times, riders on horses would take mail from place to place. That was the Pony Express."

"I would just use a phone!" said Tony.

"There were no phones back then," said Mom.

"Pony Express riders rode fast. Few riders could do it," Mom explained.

"A horse might trip in a gopher hole. A rider might hit a tree limb!" Mom said.

Tony had an idea! He stuck his thumb up and yelled, "Yes!" Then he left the den.

Tony was back. He had an old hat.

"I am the Tony Express!" he said. Mom smiled.

Mom wrote a note. "Can the Tony Express take this to Gramps?" she asked. Tony nodded.

"Look out for gopher holes and tree limbs!" Mom yelled.

The Tony Express started his ride. He climbed down high steps.

Tony's horse was strong. A wrong step might mean a bad fall.

Tony knocked twice. Knock, knock. "I am the Tony Express! I have mail," said Tony.

The note said, "Please lend me a wrench!"
Gramps grinned. "Thank you, rider," he said.

Would Tony get the wrench to Mom?
Yes! He was the Tony Express!